Lest We Forget

Books coming soon from Otis Teague

Journey Home
Love Is
Caged Love
Crime to War
BC Spy Series

Lest We Forget

*Straight Talk about Life and Faith in
times of War, Poverty and Loss of Hope.*

Second Edition

Otis Teague

Lest We Forget is a work of Non-fiction.

Scripture quotations marked KJV are from the Holy Bible, King James Version (Authorized Version). First Published in 1611. Quoted from the KJV Classic Reference Bible, Copyright © 1983 by The Zondervan Corporation.

Scripture quotations marked NASB are taken from the New American Standard Bible®, Copyright © 1960, 1962, 1963, 1968, 1971, 1972, 1973, 1975, 1977, 1995 by The Lockman Foundation. Used by permission.

Visit OMT's Images provided by Copyright Owner. Images available www.inspiredpress. shutterfly.com

Visit Author's website: www.oteague.com

Follow Otis Teague at
https://twitter.com/authorspage1
https://www.goodreads.com/authorspage1
Books and material also available at these online book stores:
www.amazon.com
www.barnesandnoble.com
www.kobo.com

Print information available on the last page.

Rev. date: 10/21/2015

To order additional copies of this book, contact:
Xlibris
1-888-795-4274
www.Xlibris.com
Orders@Xlibris.com
727583

Contents

Contents

"Purpose draws potential, potential brings to life destiny. Understanding you have a purpose is the first brick on the road to Destiny!" —Otis Teague

I dedicate this book in memory of my loving mother who spent a lifetime helping others.

Reviews of "Lest We Forget"

5 Stars- Understand - YOU have a Purpose!
Kindle Edition
"I enjoyed this book! I love it when believers step out and share their spiritual journeys and the truths they've learned along the way. It's so important AND it's scriptural!! Oral Roberts told Charles Capps years ago to never stop sharing his experiences because they are windows people can see through. I so agree with that. There are stories people need to hear so that they can SEE that God is alive, good, and not only for us but also has a unique plan for each of our lives. I appreciate the truths and the transparency in this book and join Mr. Teague in the hopes it will truly bless others as well! Thank you for sharing your journey with us!"

5 Stars-
Format: Kindle Edition
"**I was given a free copy of this book in exchange for a fair and honest review**
Lest We Forget is a book that explores the Church's role in a changing world, a world of turmoil and conflict, a world that seems to be abandoning God, a world ever more needing of hope. The author explores human motivations and the folly of capitalism, and how the void we try to fill with material things can only really be filled by the love of God. There are many

important lessons to be learnt from this book, but perhaps the biggest lesson is to look into our hearts, to think for ourselves, and to see the self-evident truths of our humanity. We have sadly let ourselves become too distracted by pettiness, and the consequences of this have been far from petty, but a better world is still within our grasp.

I particularly enjoyed how the author has shared his own experiences with absolute honesty, and this helped his messages to resonate all the more. Lest We Forget is masterfully written, and gripping from start to finish. It is the kind of book you will treasure, and read again and again."

5 Stars- You will Love this Book!
Format: Kindle Edition
"Great Inspirational Book! Well on the way to the Best Sellers list."

5 Stars- Like Fresh Manna from Heaven
Format: Hardcover
"Lest We Forget is one of those books that you will not want to put down. Like fresh manna from heaven, the book is masterfully and beautifully written, full of wise counsel, filled with life changing applications and is simply a blessing to read. This book is a faith builder that will help to guide you into greater depths of God's plans and purposes for your life. "Lest We Forget" shares pearls that open doors to kingdom principles and truths that will enable you to live a prosperous and abundant life through the simplicity of the understanding of who you are in Christ and the gifts that God has blessed you with. The author (Otis Teague) brings to the forefront from personal experience that all knowledge begins with God, His living Word and God's plans and purposes in our lives. This book will enable every reader to take hold of powerful kingdom truths."

5 Stars- Excellent; Inspirational and Insightful Look into Life & Faith

Format: Kindle Edition| Verified Purchase

"Lest We Forget" is an excellent inspirational book. I used to be afraid to admit that I have a difficult time interrupting and understanding the words of the bible. 'Lest We Forget' contains elements of the author's personal life and examples that help me understand God's words and thus allows me to place them and incorporate them into my own life. This book is an excellent tool that can be used in bible study and by many groups seeking insightful words of wisdom about Life and Faith. This book has touched my spirit and is one that I am certain I will reference and read many times."

5 Stars- Great Book on Several Levels.

Format: Kindle Edition

"I received an advanced copy of this book and thought it was wonderful. Otis Teague reminds us all about what it means to be a Christian, but he goes beyond that. He speaks from his heart and his own experience about his many personal challenges, including PTSD, and how he overcomes obstacles every day as a man of faith. I thank Teague for his military service. Read this book--it will inspire you!"

About the Book

A theologian or someone claiming to have some mystical insight into the spiritual world did not write this book. A simple guy who decided to share his experience as a Christian in his everyday walk with Christ wrote it. My Christian walk has not always been easy, but it has never been more than I could bear. We never think about that while we are going through events in our lives, even though our Christian friends whisper in our ears these comforting words. It may take you some time to realize life cannot overwhelm you unless you let it.

We may not all have the same experiences, but we all have a story to tell. Every day begins another page in the book of your life, and your story is just as important as any other story. I felt I wanted to write mine and I pray it will help someone. It's another means of reaching out to others, saved or unsaved, in hopes they may find encouragement, peace or comfort. It's my hope readers learn God exists and Jesus Christ is waiting for them to respond to the Good News that he wants to rescue them from their sins. Jesus does not force himself on people, but each person must invite him into their heart and life. Christ wants to dwell in each believer and guide him or her through the remaining pages of their book of life. Christ wants to teach and show each person that:

No height, nor depth, nor any other creature,
shall be able to separate us from the love of God,
which is in Christ Jesus our Lord. — *Romans 8:39*

The only thing that could keep us from following Christ's teaching and example is ourselves. I know we all have gone through something that causes us to ask the question why certain things happen. Sometimes we get answers, sometimes we don't. This is when you can write down the events of your life, as I began to do. In this book, I share some of my story as looked back on years of notes and was amazed at what I read. I felt those experiences were significant enough to share with others. They expressed in words how blessed I was, and I want to tell the world. If this book touches the life of just one person, then the effort has been well worth it.

We are living in a world much different than the one many of us grew up in. It has changed significantly in a relatively short time. It seems many people who once were striving to separate themselves from reality now have to face it head on. At the same time, Satan is seeking to destroy the lives of every individual on earth, as he has for thousands of years. When the people of this world tried to deal with the acts of evil, they often looked to the church for answers. It could be something as simple as asking the church to pray for our nation or pray about a personal situation. This is still happening in some areas I am sure, but it seems so subtle now, as if the church is an underground entity.

I always thought the church was a force with which to be reckoned, not some underground group. Where can the people of this world turn for help if not the church?

Introduction

Is the church the world's only hope?

Sometimes I do not think Christians understand that we play a serious role on earth. Many people have lost hope of things getting better in their lives. They do not have hope in their own lives, in their government, and they particularly don't expect the church can bring about positive change. It is as if injuries have sidelined the church. With talk of scandals, financial indebtedness, and other allegations, the "facts" have obscured the truth. With lost hope come lost dreams, untapped potential, despair, and most of all, loss of faith. Reality TV shows have become popular across the country, many times depicting the lives of those who have no hope or faith. They are bad role models, especially for people who have a saving knowledge of Christ.

Most of the time people complicate their own lives. That seems strange. What role could our relationship with God play in the world's state of being? How big of an impact will it play in the generations to come as the voice of the church seems to weaken? How do we deal with our youth who are becoming more and more programmed to the worldly standard? It may seem okay now, but what happens when we awake and realize what has happened? How many souls will be lost?

Chapter 1

What's Your Answer?

"How is your relationship with God?" Christians are often asked questions like that. People who ask those questions have a preconceived notion of what they think the answer is, and they normally base it on what they know about you.

We all think about our answer in hopes we have one. However, some like to think their relationship with God is personal and keep the answer to themselves. Others share what their relationship with God is like. Why would we keep the answer to ourselves? Is it because we think we see through the asker's intent and know the answer will have no meaning for him or her? Could it be just someone being nosy? We all know it happens. I guess I have to ask another question: Does it really matter why they ask?

I find it hard to refrain from giving an answer when people ask me about my faith. That's because of my partnership with God. I believe each Christian has a partnership with the Lord and part of that partnership is sharing a concern and love for the lost, those who do not have a personal relationship with Jesus Christ. That partnership does not tear down our wall of privacy or personal boundaries, but instead allows for open communication. Christ lives in and works through us and we are his instruments to get the work done. Our work is reaching out to people to draw them toward Christ. Sometimes that means bringing them into an environment in which they can hear clearly, and sometimes that means we have to carry them within arm's reach of the Lord.

I don't believe this world was meant to be saved, only the people in it. Somehow we have lost track of the idea we will not to be here forever and we need to decide to make maximum use of the limited time God has given us.

We have been overwhelmed with change and it is hard to keep up with it. New technologies emerge every day, and, in many instances, technological advances have made us less conscious of the shortness of time. The pace of life quickens in our dash to make or save money. I'm not against technology, but it has affected our lives in dramatic ways.

I love that God has given us so much knowledge and that we have taken advantage of it. Technology has saved the lives of countless people who had encountered illnesses. We have put in place systems allowing us to monitor processes that help humanity, such as the drug approval system administered by the Federal Drug Administration (FDA).

The FDA provides results from tested pharmaceuticals, but when you look at television commercials today, you see numerous claims about drugs that can cure certain medical conditions. However, many of the potential side effects far outweigh their ability to heal without causing any harm. We wonder how new diseases develop. I believe the very drugs we take to heal us create these new diseases. Imagine years of using untested drugs or partially tested drugs without knowing the harm to come decades later.

A system for testing drugs is crucial. But I extend my word of caution to raise the question, "Why do we blame God when things go wrong?" One answer could be "God created everything." Yet, we have manipulated some of what he created, so we must accept some of the responsibility and blame. We are still experimenting with God's creation. I am not saying we should stop looking for answers, but where we seek those answers is the key. I believe the cure to every disease we have ever encountered is here on earth and within our ability to develop.

So why haven't we discovered these cures yet? The answer to that question lies with God. He knows the right mix and dose of ingredients to create the right vaccine for any disease found here on earth. Yet, instead of seeking his answers, we blame him for our mistakes and mishaps. It's like a never-ending story, one that never seems to stop and may be purposely continued as some form of deception. Have we manipulated things so much we have lost sight of why we exist? Have we lost sight of the truth that people matter?

As Christians, we should be excited about sharing the awe-inspiring relationship we can have with Christ. Jesus never said the work would be easy or we would understand everything that happens on our journey. When our work as Christians becomes too much for us, it is usually our mindset, not the work itself, which is the root of the problem. We are human, so we tend to look at the physical side of situations and we get discouraged. Instead, we need to look on the spiritual side and be encouraged. When we look at people who show no signs of change, we get discouraged. That is another example of bearing a burden that is not ours to bear. The Lord changes people, not us. We are just his instruments.

It is human nature to want immediate change. However, we need to place that burden on Jesus Christ because he asked us to do that. Once we have done our part in reaching out to people, then we must allow Christ to do his part. Yes, that task can be hard at times. With so many distractions, so much noise from what's going on in the world—killings, robberies, financial concerns, and so many other things—it's easy to retreat to our familiar human way of looking at life. Nevertheless, we must learn to see things from God's perspective.

People are trying to do too much in too short a time. The pace makes it hard to catch ourselves and slow down our thoughts. Christians do not have to pick up that pace because it's only when we slow down we can see what is going on. We need to take time to hear what the Lord is saying to us. It's only when we clear our heads of all the noise around us that we can hand off our burdens to Christ. To get to that place is a worthy accomplishment. Only then can we begin to lessen our load and hear God say, "Allow me."

> *Come onto me all ye that labor and are heavy laden, and I will give you rest. Take my yoke upon you and learn of me; for I am meek and lowly in heart: and ye shall find rest unto your souls. For my yoke is easy, and my burden is light.* — Matthew 11: 28-30

Christians should understand the pressure is not on us. The pressure is on God. When we act on our own, we are left managing a mess. And it's the mess we created. If God has given you a job to do, you must do it. He is expecting you to do your part. He will not let any harm come to you, no matter who does not like you or what they try to do to you. You were placed there by God, and our God does not make moves just for the sake of making moves. He has strategically placed you to do a particular job. In your place of employment, for example, it could be in preparation for a blessing he wants to give you, others, or the entire company. God has embodied a certain gift within you, and it is your responsibility to see it through. Have confidence that you are in the right company at the right time and are doing God's will.

> *So shall my word be that goeth forth out of my mouth: it shall not return unto me void, but it shall accomplish that which I please, and it shall prosper in the thing whereto I sent it.* — Isaiah 55:11

This idea affects many areas of our lives. We often overlook this as we try to create our own success stories. God has spoken promises and blessing into your life and they are well worth reading in the Bible. I believe God's Word resides in a spiritual realm, unseen by us, working on the believer's behalf. I know some of you will say, "Yes I have heard that before but have yet to believe it." It's not until you believe it that you will experience the results of that belief. Even when you look at the universe, scientists are making new discoveries because the universe is still growing. Likewise, the Word of God is still working and on your behalf if you believe it. If God says something is yours, it does not matter who speaks against it. It's a matter of what you believe and what you say about it. If you believe it lines up with the Word of God, then God goes to work to make it happen.

(As it is written, I have made thee a father of many nations,) before him whom he believed, [even] God, who quickeneth the dead, and calleth those things which be not as though they were. — Romans 4:17

God will move people in great authority to deliver to you what he promised. I hear examples of that all the time: federal and state laws and rules being created and other laws being changed. Some are changed on a temporary basis, in effect just long enough for a few to be blessed by it. Some are changed completely and many people are blessed by that.

You may have wanted a house but you were not sure how you would get it. However, you knew that God has said this was the house for you. The house may be occupied at the moment, but, trust me, if God spoke it then you hold on to that and you will see the Word go to work to get you that house. It may take some time, but let patience work her perfect work. Don't try to do it on your own and only make the moves God tells you to make. You will see something wonderful happen. The family occupying the house may not even know why they have a desire to move; it could be they are moving into a bigger house, or possibly scaling down. Whatever the reason, it's all working together for the welfare of those who love the Lord. Who knows, the occupants of the house could be believers too! It could also be the house is on the market. In that case, when you speak the Word of God, the Word goes to work to find a home. The Word of God could be positioning the right realtor, right broker, and right banker. There are so many aspects to how things happen through the Word. It is often hard to know the spiritual workings going on behind the scenes. As crazy as it all may seem, things are happening by God's will, and he does it on behalf of the believer.

I experienced this sort of thing firsthand while stationed in Germany. A young soldier had brought his family to Germany with him. His wife was not working and they had three children. I got to know this young man since we were in the same military unit and work location. We worked in different sections of the building, but we saw each other often. There were times on the weekend when I would see him and his family out and about, and they were nice people. I was also aware he did not have a car to get to work and he was carpooling from some distance away.

Before I tell you what happened with the young soldier, let me say that one day going back to the base I happened to see a vehicle parked inside of a impound lot. I drove over to look at it. It was nice and I wanted to know more about it. The phone number of the owner was in the car's window, so I wrote it down, planning to buy it if I could.

Now back to the young soldier. One day the young man was in my office chatting with some of the guys who worked for me. I overheard part of their conversation—the young man was asking if they knew of anyone who was selling a car because he needed one for his family. I chimed in and said, "Hey, if you are serious about purchasing a vehicle, I have one that I might be willing to sell you."

I mentioned how I had put some money in the car and that it ran great. It was parked outside the gate, so he went and looked at it. He said it would be perfect for his family. He asked me how much I wanted for it. I had no idea at the time, so I told him let me think about a fair price. I went home and prayed about it. I laugh as I look back on that because I was praying about what would be a reasonable price for the car. The answer God gave me was a shock!

God told me the car was to be free to the family. Can you believe that? Free! I laughed at myself thinking, "God, are you sure you want me to just give the car to the young man and his family?" Finally, I said, "Okay Lord, it's free since that's what you want me do."

The young soldier was anxious to know the price, and he called me on the weekend and asked if I could drive the car to his house so his wife could look at it. I drove to their home and showed the car to his wife. She liked it too. They both asked me about the price and I said, "How about free?"

He said, "You have to let me give you something for it." I said no, I could not take any money for it. On Monday, he got insurance on the car, I canceled mine, and we changed the car over to his name.

I started driving my other car to work, and on the way back from lunch one day, I looked over to the impound yard to see if the vehicle I liked so much was still there. I figured it would not hurt to call the owner and ask if how much he was asking for the car. I called the number and the gentleman who answered the phone was not the owner but a friend of the owner who had a power of attorney to sell the vehicle. He said the owner had left the military and was interested in selling car for $2,500. He suggested I call the owner because he might lower the price.

I called the owner and discussed the car and the work he had done to it. He mentioned the one thing he had not done was replace the parking brake. I asked him how much he wanted for the car since it was exactly what I wanted since I arrived in Germany. The gentleman said, "Sir, if you are really interested in the car, you can have it for free." He told me since leaving the military he now owns three cars and the car I wanted was something lingering over his head. He wanted to get rid of it so he could have his name removed from the German DMV system.

I was speechless, I mean totally speechless. The owner said he would call his friend and authorize him to transfer ownership to me. I met the friend the next day and he said, "I don't know what you told the owner, but he said to give you the car. Many people have been trying to get this car and he turned them down because he was not sure what he was going to do with it. It's strange he's giving it to you, but I am glad you got the car."

I did my part in getting the insurance and had the car changed over to my name. Everyone at work was blown away when I drove up in a 1986 midnight gloss black Porsche 944 in excellent condition. The only repair I needed to do was the parking brake. No one could believe I paid nothing for the car, but I gave God the glory. The Porsche came to me because I had trusted God. It was an increase in faith and I could only cling to the spiritual principle I had just experienced firsthand. The blessing of God was real to me. I sowed a car and reaped an even better car. It was the kind of car I had wanted for a long time, and it was free. I often wondered what would have happened if I had sold my old car. Would the owner of the Porsche have given it to me if I had not acted in obedience and faith when I gave my car to the young soldier and his family?

Chapter 2

Authority of Your Words

I am aware that such incidents happen to people who are not Christians. Could it be due to the prayers of a family member or a believer somewhere with whom they have come in contact? I have an even better question. Is God's Word limited to the believer, or are his principles accessible to anyone who wants to use them? For example, if an unbeliever attends a church service and pays tithes, does the principle of sowing and reaping activate the Word on their behalf and generate the return promised by the Word of God? I would be interested to hear the various answers I know that question would generate.

I don't think so. God blesses those who put their faith in him.

After my eye opening experience, I see it every step of the way in life. I never want to miss an encounter that might allow me to help someone, because that incident sheds light on what happens when you get it right and benefit from the power of God's Word. No one could convince me it does not work.

I believe words have authority on earth just as I have been taught. What you say carries with it a power you cannot see, but you can often see their effects. That's why it is so important for us to be slow to speak and quick to listen. Once words leave our lips we cannot take them back. They will accomplish what they were set out to do. They will make an impact somewhere.

> *O generation of vipers, how can ye, being evil, speak good things? For out of the abundance of the heart the mouth speaketh.* — *Matthew 12:34-36*

> *Death and life [are] in the power of the tongue: and they that love it shall eat the fruit thereof.* — *Proverbs 18:21*

Imagine you're upset with someone and you say something hurtful or wish something ill against a person, and later something bad happens to them. There is death and life in the power of the tongue. You can ask them to forgive you, but you will never be able to take those words back.

If you want to experience some serious changes in your life, try speaking and putting the Word of God into practice every day of your life. Begin to pray for the people in your community, the schools and teachers in your neighborhood, and the businesses around you. Make a list of people and things to pray for and use it during a daily prayer time.

I have heard about people praying that God would remove certain people from their position or business because of their demeanor. I think it is more important to pray for them to come to know Christ. You may think they will never change. You don't know, and by doubting, you have limited the power of God's Word. Even though you may not see a change, that does not mean it is not taking place. It could be years before they change, but you best believe that if you have prayed from your heart for that person, something is taking place within their life.

> *And being fully persuaded that, what he had promised, he was able also to perform.* — *Romans 4:21*

We have to be fully persuaded and not be moved by how things may look. We must understand God is faithful and every word that he speaks is true.

I will worship toward thy holy temple, and praise thy name for thy loving-kindness and for thy truth: for thou hast magnified thy word above all thy name. — Psalms 138:2

Think about that for a moment. If you have recently received Christ as your Lord and Savior, it may just sound like words. I beg you give Christ a chance! You will see that he will come through for you. I have been there! Who hasn't? People of faith get down to the wire sometimes, and that's when the door opens. There have been times when I would think something is not for me, or I begin to think what I did wrong. But when the door opens, I realize God has shown me I was not where I thought I was in believing and trusting Him. Such incidents teach us about ourselves, the strength of our faith, and how God works in our lives. That does help keep us grounded and from deceiving ourselves.

Be mindful that his timing does not always line up with our timing. Most of the time, it never will be. We learn through repetition. With every encounter, test, and trial, we learn to believe in Christ and his power even more. It's our job to believe God will do his job, and, when you reach that point, you will begin to apply the Word of God to your own situations. In essence, you are growing up in Christ, and it's a feeling unlike any other you have experienced. I encourage you to keep yourself free by repenting every day for your sins, known and unknown.

If we confess our sins, he is faithful and just to forgive us our sins, and to cleanse us from all unrighteousness. —1 John 1:9

No matter how long you have walked with Christ, you need to know the boundaries he has set forth.

- Don't try to figure out how God will deal with a situation or how he will work it out. God's timing is the unknown factor when it comes to how he is going to work something out. You may be impatient. This is likely to cause you unwanted stress. Simply open your ears, eyes, and mind, and listen for that still small voice and his presence will reassure you. God understands and he will give you instructions if he has any.

- Don't look at your current circumstances, because if Christ is in it, it will most likely change. Faith can increase regardless of your circumstances. Think about where your faith would be if you knew every circumstance you would face. Rather, think on the endless possibilities when you don't know, but believe God is in control. The possibilities are endless because you are a child of the Most High God.

- Don't allow your emotions to drive or provoke you. Keeping our emotions in check is by far the hardest thing to do. We are human, and at times we are driven by our emotions. Men and women have an intuitive instinct that triggers emotional responses. Unchecked, this has put some people in some tough spots because emotions can generate improper actions. I believe the act of adultery starts out that way. A man sees (eyes) a beautiful woman, an image of that woman produces a thought (mind). That thought triggers an emotion (heart) which triggers an action. Women react to their emotions in this way too.

A good man out of the good treasure of his heart brings forth good; and an evil man out of the evil treasure of his heart[a] brings forth evil. For out of the abundance of the heart his mouth speaks. — Luke 6:45

What happens if what we see is not what it seems to be? What if you move falsely from the place God has placed you? Imagine how much that could throw you off course, and who knows but God the impact of such an error? Don't be conformed to your current situation, but be transformed. It's only by the renewing of your mind that we can begin to see things through the eyes of God.

Now the question is, "Can I see things through the eyes of God? After all, God is in heaven and I am down here on earth." Let's look at the process. First, let's break down the word "repent." The prefix "Re" – means to turn or go back. Back where? The word "pent" is where we get our word penthouse, a high place of dwelling. So, when a person repents they go back to their high place of dwelling.

If you live in a house with only one floor, you are limited by your surroundings to seeing what's around you. You can see what is across the street from you, the house behind you, and maybe even a few houses down the street. Without the ability to see beyond those houses, or further down the street, it's impossible to determine what is taking place beyond those areas.

Now let's look at the view from a penthouse. Most penthouses have many windows with multiple views. The view allows you to see for great distances. As you walk around your penthouse, you can look down and see more than you could at ground level. From your penthouse, you can see local places you want to visit. You also have the perspective to see how difficult it is to get there because of traffic and congestion. That is a fine analogy because when we repent we are placed in a rightful place with God, which often allows us to see things from a penthouse view. We can get God's perspective on things when we have faith in him and his methods.

People are continually looking for answers. At one time, they sought the answers within the church. When times got tough, they often sought refuge inside the church. They could hear the voice of the church through the strife of the world. It was a place of peace. People knew the church was a place with answers and a place that would equip them to deal with whatever warfare may be taking place in their life. Has the church continued to be a refuge from the strife of this world? I am sure the answers will vary here too. The role of local churches has changed in the minds of people. So, how do we approach the issues and concerns facing the people of this world? I know that hoping the concerns of the world will simply pass us by isn't the answer. We must place our faith in Jesus Christ.

Churches are not like the little boy who throws a stone and then hides his hand. The church stands and says, "This is why we threw the stone." When laws are passed that we know are ethically and morally corrupt, local churches must take a stand. I believe churches are like a U.S. embassy, but on a much greater scale. God has strategically placed them and staffed them with those whom he has called according to his purpose. Many things can outlive their usefulness, but the church is not one of them.

Pastors are like ambassadors. We often hear that we are all ambassadors of Christ. I believe we are ambassadors from heaven. However, we have to understand something about ambassadors; they do not come with their own message, but carry the message of the one who sent them.

The message is not the same for each ambassador, but they all have the same goal. The goal is to minister to the broken-hearted, reach out to the lost, and build up the Kingdom of God. We cannot afford to get away from that. Our moves should be orchestrated by God and not our own intentions. Remember, God did not place us here on earth to simply exist and die, nor are we here for our own selfish gains. It's all about God and his love for what he has created. It's about sharing God's love and drawing the lost to Jesus Christ, our Savior. It's about reaching PEOPLE!

I often had dreams and visions and I would write down what I could recall. No, I do not claim to have a spiritual gift in that regard, but God can speak to us in different ways.

Once I had a dream about heaven, and I recall people standing in this line in front of God. He was speaking to each person individually by whispering in their ear. Everyone else in line was staring and wondering what God was asking the person. After giving an answer, each person walked away and could not speak to anyone else in line. It turned out the question was "What did you do with the gift and time I gave you?"

We should be making a difference by making use of the gifts and time God has given us. He may call us before him to answer that question at any moment. I don't think any of us will have the perfect answer. However, we must think about how we use the gifts and the time God has given us now so that we will be ready to give an answer later.

Our answer may be short or long. The reality is God already knows what we have done with our gifts and time. You now have the opportunity to get a start on answering that question for yourself. Would the answer sound anything like this: "Lord, I did not receive any gifts" or "I did not know how to use the gifts, because you never taught me." If you don't like that answer, you have the opportunity to work on things you would be proud to report. Make sure you use your gifts and time in line with God's Word.

Maybe God will ask us if we have shared the relationship we have with Christ with anyone. We may only remember a few. I am not talking in numbers because you can never know what that number might be. For example, the impact you have on one person could be shared by numerous others through that one person. The chain reaction of sharing could go on for years. You may never know the number of people you influenced in a positive spiritual way. Sometimes your story of how you were drawn to Christ is what echoes down through time.

In this book, you will learn that you have a story to tell and it may help you draw the lost to Christ. You need to share your faith in a style that fits you. You do not have to put on an act; people can usually see through that. Putting on an act will weaken your effectiveness. God has made you a unique person and you must share the "real you" with others.

Reaching people for Christ— learning to share your faith— is a lifestyle. It is part of the everyday Christian life. It cannot be separated from Christianity. The Christian faith is about sharing with others and helping them. It is not about getting all you can. That would be no different from the way non-Christians live their lives.

Chapter 3

People Matter

I ask you to use your imagination as you read this book. Close your eyes and see my word images in your mind. Picture you are a child who has wandered off from your parents and you are lost. You have no recollection of where they are. Stop there.

Now imagine you are the parents of that child who has wandered off. As an adult you know the dangers of being lost, alone, and afraid.

Both situations are very scary, but this happens every day in our world. The parents call the police and then call everyone they know, asking if they had seen their child. They drive every street looking for their child and post flyers everywhere. Parents never give up searching until they find their child.

Though the child is lost and afraid, he or she may come across something they may find amusing or someone who may befriend them. Both are a temporary comfort and may take the child's mind off what they are feeling for a moment. In contrast, the parents are still as worried and afraid as they were when the child first disappeared. They never stop loving their child even though they are separated.

Is it possible God sees the lost in a similar way? Jesus tells three parables in Luke 15. God has gone to great lengths to allow us to see how much he cares about us no matter how lost we may be.

The first parable deals with the shepherd who left 99 sheep to go after the one lost sheep. The parable signifies there is great value in the one sheep that is lost.

> *What man of you, having an hundred sheep, if he lose one of them, doth not leave the ninety and nine in the wilderness, and go after that which is lost until he find it. — Luke 15:4*

The second story speaks of the woman who lost a coin and cleaned her house from corner to corner looking for it. What importance does this coin have? It had value to the woman.

> *And when she hath found it, she calleth her friends and her neighbors together, saying, rejoice with me; for I have found the piece which I had lost. Luke 15:8-9*

The last and very familiar story is of the prodigal son who asked his father for his inheritance. Then he left home to squander it, having what he thought was a good time. The father was hurt for he had great love for his son. Let's read the story as Luke tells it:

> *A certain man had two sons: And the younger of them said to his father, Father, give me the portion of goods that falleth to me. And he divided unto them his living. And not many days after the younger son gathered all together, and took his journey into a far country, and there wasted his substance with riotous living. And when he had spent all, there arose a mighty famine in that land; and he began to be in want.*

"And he went and joined himself to a citizen of that country; and he sent him into his fields to feed swine. And he would fain have filled his belly with the husks that the swine did eat: and no man gave unto him. And when he came to himself, he said, How many hired servants of my fathers have bread enough and to spare, and I perish with hunger!

I will arise and go to my father, and will say unto him, Father, I have sinned against heaven, and before thee, and am no more worthy to be called thy son: make me as one of thy hired servants. And he arose, and came to his father. But when he was yet a great way off, his father saw him, and had compassion, and ran, and fell on his neck, and kissed him.

And the son said unto him, Father, I have sinned against heaven, and in thy sight, and am no more worthy to be called thy son. But the father said to his servants, Bring forth the best robe, and put it on him; and put a ring on his hand, and shoes on his feet: And bring hither the fatted calf, and kill it; and let us eat, and be merry: For this my son was dead, and is alive again; he was lost, and is found. And they began to be merry. — Luke 15:11-24

Take a closer look at these parables. In each, something of significant value was lost. The lost item was so significant it caused someone to search diligently, and in some instances reach out to others to help search. When they found what they were looking for, they had a great celebration.

Luke tells us the woman called all her friends over to celebrate. The shepherd also had a celebration. The father of the prodigal son ordered the fatted calf slain for a feast in celebration of the return of his son.

If you think about this, it sounds very much like how we would react after finding our own lost child. We too would probably phone the same friends we had asked to help look for our child and ask them to celebrate with us.

These three parables touch my heart. I prayed over these Scriptures and as I began to study them for the third time, the voice of God spoke to me saying "Fear not."

I knelt and the Lord asked "Will you help them find me?"

I said "Yes." At that moment I had no clue about what that meant in detail, but I was not about to refuse.

He then said, "Remind them that I love them and that they matter to me. It does not matter what they have done. I will forgive them because I love them. I love them more than they will ever know. They may not understand this love, but they will come to understand it."

"Yes! Yes! Lord," I replied, and I began to worship him.

Then the voice said to me, "I will provide everything you need to make this happen. But understand the greater the number you reach the greater the opposition will be. Remember not to worry about things, but focus on the lost."

It was from that point on that those Scriptures burned in my heart, as if God had placed his hand over my heart and branded those words on it. I knew God wanted me to remember forever his words.

I understood why my heart constantly reached out to people. Communicating and bringing people together was a small task for me. Befriending people came easy for me, as if it were an art. Growing up on the south side of Chicago, in a neighborhood surrounded by gangs, drugs, and poverty, was never easy. I had developed a talent for persuading others. It seemed as if they wanted to hear what I had to say, even though the stares I sometimes got were weird. I use to say things like, "There has to be something better out here in this world," and that caused some to think I was odd.

Now I understand the gift God had given me. I used it for the wrong reasons growing up. The enemy had deceived me, as he does everyone who is not spiritually aware. He will convince you that you will never be anything, and there is no need to move beyond your current state of being.

I know there are many people who live their entire life in the same environment, not recognizing there is hope beyond life as they know it. I also realize it can be hard to get perspective when there is no hope around you. The truth is far from that; even if you are living on the street, there is hope. Even if you have lost everything, there is hope.

Poor people are not the only ones who despair. Many times those who have everything they want in life can reach a point of despair. They get a periodic feeling that something is missing. They may not say anything and may attempt to hide it, but I can promise you they feel it at times. It's during those moments of being alone when things are silent, in those moments of stillness they feel this despair the most. They may not understand what is happening or why they feel empty. They may try to fill that void with alcohol or drugs, but they can only try to fill that void for so long. They discover nothing physical will be able to fill it. The wise ones learn that rich or poor, only Jesus Christ can fill the void they feel.

The power of the Word of God is SO AMAZING! It is SO POWERFUL! Watch someone undergoing a spiritual transformation and you can see by their expression or gestures that the Word is making a remarkable impact in their lives.

Parents play an important role in imparting values to their children. Parents have such a brief time with their children. Everyone knows how important it is for parents to spend time teaching their children right from wrong, but Christian parents know they need to do more than that. They must impart the Word of God into their child's life.

I believe that regardless of the environment, if a child grows up receiving the Word of God in their home or church, the Word remains in them. Though the Word has been shared with them and is in them, we also have to remember God has given all men and women the power of human choice. When children come of age, they will have to accept responsibility for the decisions they make. Will they make mistakes? Yes, but hopefully they will learn from them. Parents must have confidence that they have implanted values in their children that may someday save their life. Never think that all is lost; never give up on your son or daughter. Let them know that you love them unconditionally. What you taught them about praying before they go to bed will stick with them when they get older. What you shared with them during your talks at the breakfast or dinner table is a part of them.

What happens when the child ends up committing a crime or their life does not go the direction the parents hoped it would? I heard the story of one parent praying to God after her son had been saved. She prayed God would call him home (die) if God knew that her child would go back to drugs or committing crimes again. I assume that this way she at least would know he is with God and she would see him again.

I know I tried to make excuses with my mother when I was growing up. She would simply say, "You know better than that." I would agree; often knew I was wrong and had a look of shame. It simply boils down to an individual decision. People choose to do what they feel is right for them in their current situation. They do not consider the effects of their decisions; sometimes the ramifications can be bad and they see no way back.

God has given us gifts to be used throughout the earth for his glory. After reading this book, you may discover you possess some of God's gifts. These gifts are critical assets for our time on earth. I know the enemy Satan is jealous of these gifts. He acknowledges the gifts exist and people possess them, but the deception comes in having you believe the gifts are to be used as you wish as in material gain rather than spiritual gain. Satan wants you to use your gifts for gaining wealth and fame rather than glorifying God.

Still, there are those who use their gifts to help others as much as they can, and that is laudable. I do not believe God meant a select few to carry this burden; when one person helps another using their spiritual gifts, kindness spreads like a contagious disease. There is enough wealth in the world to support every individual on this planet if people shared it.

One of the hardest things for us to do after receiving Jesus Christ as Lord and Savior is to move beyond our past— letting go of the "old man" as they say. It's hard for people to leave their comfort zone, the environment with which they are most familiar. It's not that we don't want to or can't do it—sometimes it's the fear of leaving the familiar and entering the realm of the unfamiliar. For me, when I received Christ, I would always think about who I was now and how I was supposed to act. It is all a learning process. Some churches have classes for new Christians which is tremendous. It is hard to fight the person you once where, and other Christians can help you in the battle. They can help new Christians overcome habits and temptations so the struggle to defeat them is not so difficult. I think we lose some new Christian believers as they struggle with leaving their old way of living. Christians can help their brothers and sisters in Christ from venturing back to the familiar.

You will make mistakes. However, what's important is that you keep trying and not give up. The Lord will help you. Christianity does not rest on feelings. Sometimes you won't feel saved, but don't give in to that feeling. It's just a feeling! It's not enough that some new believers think they are not saved anymore if they make a mistake or struggle with a bad habit. Sadly, some Christians make them feel bad because they are not perfect. Yes, new believer, some Christians make the mistake of making you feel that way, and sometimes it is unintentional. Find the right church, pray, and know the gift is from God and only he can take it away. Your gift belongs to you as long as you want it, and as long as you continue to use it as God instructs you.

Gifts God has given us are another area where we often lose focus. We tend to stop using the gifts, especially if we believe the old cliché that to be humble you have to be poor, or at least living a life that shows no sign of prosperity. We should realize by now God is not going to take back the gifts he provides. The Bible says:

> *The gifts and the calling of God are irrevocable.*
> — *Romans 11:29*

For example, when I received Jesus Christ as my Lord and Savior I stopped reaching out to people. I somehow became a different person and did not want to get involved with people who did not understand what God was doing in my life. I did not realize I needed to continue to reach out. The difference should be in the way I would speak to everyone about how God was changing my life. We should all be excited and passionate about our new life in Christ.

The book of Acts sheds light on this when it talks about Saul before he became known as the Apostle Paul. Saul persecuted Christians, killing them by the thousands before his life-changing encounter with God.

> *And he fell to the earth, and heard a voice*
> *saying unto him, Saul, Saul why persecute thou*
> *persecute me?* — *Acts 9:4*

Later the Apostle Paul reached out to them, drawing and protecting them with the same diligence he once used to kill them. We can learn a lot from Saul's transformation. I wonder how much could be accomplished if we maintained the same intensity level and remained as effective as when we first received Christ. We must allow God to perfect in us the gifts that glorify Him.

God can sharpen and mature your gifts. If you can reach 100 people, he will enable you to draw 1000 people. Evangelism is part of every Christian's daily ministry. Some churches hold once a month evangelism outreach, which draw hundreds and sometimes thousands of people. However, many churches fail to impart in their members their calling to have an everyday ministry to reach the lost. Each person has a sphere of influence and a Christian can reach the people in it, according to the Word of God. You can have an important impact on the people around you.

The way you interact can be a tool to draw those people to Christ. Some believe working as an evangelist is the only true way to reach people. This results from a lack of teaching about true evangelism. What do you say to someone who asks the question, "Why do I need to bother with reaching people? God already has someone for that task, and I would probably not be good at it anyway. Shouldn't I shoot for a position in the church, maybe a deacon or something?" Some Christians fail to understand that God has given us all a story to tell, and, through our stories, we can help draw the lost to Christ. All it takes is the opportunity and environment. If you can focus for a moment and genuinely share a concern for bringing the lost to Christ, the opportunities will present themselves—the right time, right moment, and right environment. God will ensure it happens. The big question is what you will do when it comes? Will you recognize the opportunity when it arises?

Chapter 4

Breaking Relationship Barriers

What are some of the growing concerns frustrating the state of the world right now? I believe one concern is the feeling of irrelevance of religion in the world. A prime example would be what has gone on in countries like Syria, other areas of the Middle East, and even in the United States. Why would individuals who claim to embrace Islam commit such horrific acts of violence in the name of a peaceful and loving God? Such violence cannot equate to the love of God in any respect.

We have seen countless acts of criminal activity, even in the religious environment. For instance, capturing individuals who are not Muslim for ransom is one such crime. What is that all about anyway? How can you say that you are fighting on behalf of what is supposedly one of the most peaceful religions in the world?

I believe education is the key to eliminating any radical religion, including radical Islam. We are all human first and the human relationship regardless of race, religion, or gender – entails mutual respect. Such respect encompasses tolerance, but not for the sake of seeking power. It seems that radical Islamic Muslims do not understand true Islam at all and many have been deceived into believing in the radical cause without truly studying the Koran for themselves. During my reading of the Koran, I found that Muslims are called to love beyond their own culture. The relationships I developed with Muslims during my tenure working overseas confirmed just that, the respect in many cases was mutual. Granted not every Muslim was or is the same, I have encountered situations that made me feel uncomfortable. Nevertheless the experience of having worked in such places as Kuwait, Dubai, Iraq, and Afghanistan will never be forgotten. With all there is to be said about religion, there is only one true God and I am not saying the voice of God has changed or fallen silent. I am asking, "Where is the amplification of the words through the heart of those who believe in God?"

With crime on the rise in nearly every state and terrorism becoming the new focus of the world, suicide is on the rise. It's alarming to hear even American citizens have left to join in fighting against our country. Can these be distractions of the enemy? I believe they are. More and more the question becomes how we deal with these distractions. I wonder if by chance we Christians had been given a message for them and it turned into a missed opportunity. These acts of violence are not the Christians' fault, but if we do not reach the perpetrators, the enemy will somehow find them.

It does not take much to plant a seed and you don't have to watch it grow. You can share your faith in a style that fits you at work, in the grocery store, at the mall, or at the gas station. It does not require a lot of changing and you don't have to try to be more than you are. There are so many instances where the opportunity arises to share an encouraging word with someone and we fail to seize the moment.

Let me encourage you to stop worrying about what people think of you. If God gives you a word to share with someone, just do it. Sometimes it may take some boldness, calling for you to take a stand. God will set the atmosphere and make sure you are in the right environment to do so. The Holy Spirit will let you know when to do it.

When we do recognize those moments of opportunity to share, we should also recognize and minimize the distractions that may hinder us from sharing. For me these are the important moments in life. My job and the sustainment of my everyday life I leave to God. I know I need to work, but God opens the door of opportunity for me to have a job. But the value I hold in reaching people carries more weight than my job. There is joy in having to get up every day to go to work because it means new opportunities.

There is someone who needs to hear your story; there is someone out there who has been waiting a lifetime to hear your story because it is the same thing they may be going through or may be getting ready to go through. God has given you a word to share, and maybe that's all they need to hear. Imagine sharing one word that could potentially change someone's life.

Think on that for a moment. Could it be that we miss opportunities that arise every day? What happens when we become conscious of that? What do we do when we realize as we leave our homes every day, this might be the day I meet someone who may be going through something and my conversation with them may hold the key to them overcoming it?

We do not always see the initial spiritual impact of our witnessing. By this, others can be delivered and drawn to Christ our Savior. Think of how those negative and positive experiences could be used to help win souls for Christ; those stories now become part of you. Think about that the next time you come out of a bad experience you feel no one else in the world could have possibly gone through. There is nothing new under the sun according to the Word of God. I use to think that meant nothing new such as inventions, but I started taking it literally. So never think no one else in the world has gone through what you have or are going through.

You may be one who likes to entertain and invite others over for dinner. What an excellent time to witness to someone. However, you must ensure you express what God has placed on your heart to share with your guest before the meal. Keep your conversation down to about 15 to 20 minutes. Most people tend to lose interest if you have not expressed the heart of what you are trying to say within that time. You have to be careful, especially if you are a fast talker. Sometimes we are so anxious to spread the Good News of Christ and all that he has done for you that we do not give the person a chance to comprehend what we are saying. For the person listening, it's like hearing a used car salesman. He speaks so fast that you can't keep up and often he talks around details that you might be interested in. So, slow down when talking with others and sharing your faith.

There are a few ways to help develop your gift and ability to reach people. You can reach them with the help of God by simply being yourself. The more you understand God's love for you, the more you will understand his love for the lost, which should cause you to want to reach them even more.

If any pastor wants his congregation to grow or increase, then your church needs to be able to reach people effectively. A maturing Christian will recognize this as growing in Christ. As much as your church can help, I think it's more important for individuals to be open as God shows them themselves, this allows them to see themselves first and help them to understand their own temperament and how to approach people. It is so important we understand ourselves. I do not understand why we complicate reaching people, when the blueprint is in the Bible.

Now going back to our partnership with God, understand partners normally share a similar interest. When we share the interest of God, we do not have to wait on the Lord to move, we can move in the interest of the Kingdom by telling people that God loves them, God cares about them, and he is asking them to give him a chance. We have to understand that reaching people is a lifestyle, just as Christianity is a lifestyle, and we are to live that life to its fullest. It cannot simply be about what God has done or can do for us, but sharing how much God loves the other person and what he has and can do for them.

Chapter 5

Step by Step

My relationship with God developed in stages; first, I had to learn to trust him. In other words, I had to fellowship with him, talk with him, and let him know how I was feeling, just as he would let me know things about him when I read his Word and worshipped him. Friendship resulted from our fellowship. Our relationship gets better every day. My trust and faith in him became stronger.

Sincere fellowship will lead to sincere friendship, and that opens the door for a relationship with those God calls you to befriend. People will sometimes question you when they see you with someone with whom they might not otherwise engage, but if that is who God has called you to speak with, then do not let the chance pass you by.

Looks can be deceiving. People have been misjudged because of the way they dress, talk, or color of their skin. I have heard Christians tell stories of places God sent them to speak with just one individual. God gave them details down to what the person would be wearing—all for that single person. I thought amazing that God would do that for one person.

Let us look at Mark 14: 3-9 where the woman anoints Jesus with oil. An ordinary woman was pouring expensive oil on Jesus' head when Judas confronted him and said, "Why do you waste such expensive ointment? Do you not know we could have sold this?" Jesus responded to him saying, "You will always have the poor with you and can help them whenever you want, but you will not always have me."

Look closer at this situation. We have disciples who traveled with Jesus day and night, spent hours with him, and prayed with him. However, God gave revelation knowledge to a woman known for sin and allowed her to anoint Jesus with oil. Therefore, do not think that you have to be a pastor, teacher, or evangelist to reach people. Our God can use anyone, and that is something I have come to love about him. The Bible overflows with examples of God using ordinary people to do extraordinary things.

People often say, "God is looking for people who will go out into the world and walk in faith." Such people are trusting that God will do what he says he will do. I can tell you that he will.

Now let me ask you "What if I was someone you trusted and I said those words to you?" I believe they would carry some weight in helping you believe God will do what he says. It's not that God needs that from us, but when people see and hear it from someone they trust then it helps build their trust factor. Someone has to go into the cities and suburbs to reach others. Someone must go to the alleys, and the different corporations and companies to reach others. In some instances, it will take boldness on the part of the Christian, but God does not make wimps.

Sometimes God may ask things that will not make sense to some people. For example, he may send two guys to stand in front of a night club until 3 in the morning handing out flyers to those going in and coming out. The flyers say, "God loves you no matter what you have done. He is constantly calling to you so you can spend eternity with him." Then, two weeks later, you see some of those same people in the church you attend. You understand then that God will do what he says he will do.

As a Christian, you have the power to draw someone to Jesus. Your spiritual self, as God has created it, embodies the power. It is normal for you to want to reach people.

The desire to reach out to others increases as you mature in Christ. Your language, your physical make-up, and where you are right now in Christ can be used to reach and encourage others. You do not have to attain a certain level in the church or have a college degree before you can become effective. Those are great to have, and I encourage you to earn a college degree because there are benefits, but remember it is only a degree of knowledge and is limited to a few subjects. Imagine when you gain the capability to tap into God, who has all knowledge about all things. If you are saved and trust God, you need never think the world has more knowledge than you have access to through God.

There was a time as a young Christian I was excited about telling others about Christ and how to accept Christ as their Lord and Savior. I had no idea of how to reach them or get my point across, but I had a strong motivation from God. All I knew was I had this excitement inside of me to tell others about what I was feeling, and God blessed that desire in my life.

As I grew in Christ, I would spend time praying and asking God how to reach people so they could see and feel what I saw and felt. Then they would know it's all real. The answer came to me in prayer. God told me to simply be myself. He wanted me to share who I am in Christ with people. I learned from my experience that not everyone who says they love Christ actually loves him. Some say they love him in their own way. I am not judging if they love him or not. That is an individual matter anyway, because Christ has a unique plan for each of us.

John 14:15 "If ye love me, keep my commandments."

There are some believers who do all they can to uphold his commandments, and we know it's a tough fight. We do not always get it right, though we have the right intentions. I believe God also looks at the intent of the heart, so he knows if we were trying to keep his commandments and somehow missed the mark. We can learn, ask forgiveness, and move on.

We cannot judge people by where they are in their Christian walk. We are all at different levels of spiritual maturity. However, we should all be growing in our faith. It is a bad sign if we are not growing and maturing. Some Christians are content with where they are in Christ. I wonder if Christ is content with them being where they are. We all need to grow in Christ on a daily basis.

The Holy Spirit is constantly trying to communicate with us. If we are listening to God's Spirit, we cannot help but grow. If we do not listen to the Holy Spirit, problems arise. We have no idea what to say or do. Our only hope is to listen to God's Spirit. Then, we do not have to feel out of place when it comes to talking and sharing with other people. The confidence comes when we hear the Holy Spirit speak to us.

Chapter 6

Being Yourself

There is an evangelistic style that fits you. When you discover it, you will feel comfortable communicating with people in any environment.

Being yourself and confident is a plus, but that confidence grows when the Holy Spirit guides you. Nevertheless, there are some cautions to consider when dealing with people. Not every individual has noble intentions and may deceive you into thinking you are helping them.

Sometimes that deception works in reverse. You may find yourself hurting someone rather than helping them. For example, God could be teaching someone who has a money problem to depend on him. You come along with good intentions and they ask to borrow a substantial amount of money from you. You agree, but they end up mismanaging that money. When they are unable to repay you, they are back to the same situation they were in initially. You may feel disturbed about it, and they may feel ashamed. Yes, this happens, but you can avoid this sort of thing by hearing what the Holy Spirit is telling you about the individual. You must be listening.

Again, our God looks at the heart. If your heart was genuine when you tried to assist someone, I believe God will honor that action and ensure you are not overtaken by anything negative. If you are concerned about retribution for the person who tried to deceive you, it is best to forget it. God is just and he takes care of those matters. Remember, whenever someone uses God's Word, it will find a place to plant itself within that individual. Even though it may not affect the person right away, the Word will remain with him or her. You may never see the impact it had on them, but God and others will. If you announce Christ here on earth, then he'll announce you before his Heavenly Father. This is what he says in the Gospel of Matthew:

> *Whosoever therefore shall confess me before men, him will I confess also before my Father which is in Heaven.* — *Matthew 10:32*

Our temperaments play a large role in how we approach people, and we must understand that any evangelistic style may cause damage if we do not take precautions. Those precautions include not allowing the conversation to go beyond what Christ has imparted in you. He sets the boundaries about what you are to share with people. Sometimes our conversations tend to venture into areas never meant to be discussed, and we lose our audience. That is not good. Jesus is interested in how we present him and ourselves to those who are lost and unsaved in this world.

When I was growing up, I witnessed the "holier-than-thou" mentality and wanted nothing to do with it. It was an impossible life to live and a setup for failure. It leaves no room for mistakes or errors, and that is not realistic because all humans are flawed. Even in our humanity, we must be careful we do not misrepresent God or Jesus Christ.

This can happen when we cease being who we are in Christ and allow the flesh (self) to surface during an encounter with someone. When we portray ourselves to be more than we are, selfish intentions can ruin the conversation. We are Spirit first, created from God himself. When we walk in that truth, he gives us a confidence no one can take away from us. Some people want to challenge that confidence. They want to put it to the test. They tend to ask that one question for which we do not have an answer. Although we may not have the answer, we can tap into one who does—God. So, the potential for you to give them an answer is there. We should not be afraid to say, "I know God has the answer to that question," and invite them to spend some time with Christ to get the answers they seek. We should not try to elude questions when we face that challenge.

> *Always be prepared to give an answer to everyone who asks you to give reason for the hope that is within you, but do this with gentleness and respect.* — *1Peter 3:15*

I love Peter's practicality in that statement. We must be prepared to give an answer. Peter makes it sound as if this is not optional or debatable. We must not miss an opportunity to influence someone's life. God's work is serious. Your readiness to have an answer depends on how much value you add to it. Reading the Word of God or even picking up a book like this one can help you prepare to share your faith.

In this Bible passage, I believe what Peter is saying is speak to them about the Christ that is in you. Share how your relationship started. Tell people when and where Christ found you. Let them know what Christ has done for you. Give examples without overwhelming them. Let them know that the Lord can do the same for them. Have something to say about how God has changed you. Your story is special and people will listen when you share it. Your story could make a life-changing difference to the person to whom you are speaking. Sometimes you may simply offer encouraging words that point the way to Christ. You may be able to share with them if they see you are kind to them even when they have been unkind to you. Win them over with love. It can be hard to love someone who seems

to be unlovable, but you can do it through the power of the
Holy Spirit.

The Scripture says anyone who asks can get an answer to
his or her questions. I like that idea. Even the guy who lives
on the street and is not well groomed is privileged to receiving
answers to questions about matters of faith and life because the
Scripture leaves no one out. In addition, nowhere does it say any
race or ethnic background is excluded from getting an answer
to their questions. So, it is up to you to follow the example of
Christ and share the Good News with all people. Speak, but be
mindful of what you say. Be slow to speak and quick to listen. If
the person you are speaking with has something to say, or wants
to share an experience, then by all means listen. Then you can
share whatever God lays on your heart either from the Bible or
your personal life experience. God uses both to heal the hearts
of the unsaved.

Chapter 7

Representing the Kingdom

People ask all kinds of questions. Sometimes they ask Bible questions, but often their questions are about how to cope with certain situations. You can give them "how-to" answers based on spiritual principles. Whenever anyone asks you a question, it is another witnessing opportunity. Everyone matters to God and everyone should matter to you too.

People watch how you react to different situations and may approach you to compliment you on it. If they are drawn to you, that's an advantage because you can then point them to Christ. When you claim to be a Christian, people tend to watch your actions and reactions closer. That's a funny thing, because before you mention anything about being a Christian, no one has any expectations about you. After they learn you are a Christian, they will want to see if your talk and walk is consistent.

The most you can expect from people is that they will listen to what you have to say. How much they will take in will be determined by what they think of you in the first place. Caring people tend to give time. Time is one of the most precious gifts in the world you can give, and you can give time to anyone.

I have always put more weight on the value of a gift when someone made it for me rather than buying it in a store. The idea of them giving their time and adding their personal touch makes a huge difference. I think listening is a gift I can give to people, so I like to show respect when people talk. People have never understood that about me. There have been times when friends have watched me talk with people with whom they would never talk. Afterwards, they would say, "OT, why do you listen to that guy? Doesn't he seem a little strange to you?" They are right— not all the conversations make sense to me, but people matter to me. I see the look in their eyes and see the expression of excitement they have when they know someone is actually listening to them. It gives me an opportunity to share my faith, my experiences, and my story. How you listen and what you say makes a difference in the lives of other people. I always want to make a positive impact in the lives of people I meet.

Earlier I said there is someone in this world that has been waiting a lifetime to hear that one word from God that will change his or her life forever. God gave that word to a Christian somewhere on earth to share. We never know when or where the conversation will take place. We do not know what type of situation in which the person may be. They could be on the verge of suicide or killing someone out of anger. They may have lost everything they ever worked for, or perhaps they are empty and alone and don't know about the love of God.

As Christians, we must be ready to help people in whatever situation we find them. I believe that is why we should always be on our best behavior—and I say that with a smile. I know we all have our moments of struggle, anger, or frustration, but we have the Lord and we can talk to him about those moments. Jesus cares and listens to us, so we need to listen to others even when we may not be at our best.

I am not saying we have to be serious all the time, because we can have fun as Christians. Think how much more the world would be separated if things were that way: all the serious

Christians this side and all the Christians who like to have fun on this side. We are often told Christianity is an individual walk. If that is true, what does it matter how my walk is different from yours? People react differently to different situations, and so we should be mindful of whom and whose we are. We represent our Father in heaven. We help by praying for others and being there for them when they need us. We must always reach out to them in fellowship, ensuring they know they are loved.

I recall a particular officer stationed with me who claimed to be a Christian. I was the type of person who was constantly making notes about my interactions as they took place. One day we were all in the office when we heard what sounded as if someone was throwing furniture around in the office next to ours. That's exactly what was happening; the officer was throwing chairs and tossing things off his desk. I was floored; it was unbelievable. He was using language far from Christian, I thought.

He did not want to talk with anyone. I remember thinking, what kind of God does he serve? People would whisper about his actions behind his back as if they saw no hope for him. Office conversations were often about the intensity of the workload. Those of us who had been working in the office over the years thought it might be time to request a change of station, because things were getting bad around there.

We found out later that his reaction was sparked by a message that his boss was not pleased with some of his work. As usual, I wrote that incident down so that I could pray about it. My prayer was simple. I asked God to open an opportunity for me to speak with him if only for a moment. I knew God would give me a word for him although it would be brief. To make a long story short, God did open up an opportunity for us to talk, and the conversation included a little bit about our faith. I believe what God gave me to share helped the officer.

I was also able to explain to him that his subordinates were looking for him to bring them together to develop solutions to the problems so he would not need to get so angry. Anger itself is not always bad, but people always remember your actions when you lose control. I remember joking with him. I said, "Hey, after kicking over the chair and slamming your hand on the desk, did your problem go away?" I reassured him that the rest of the staff faced the same pressures he faced, and we could all work through it together as a team. God will always take care of his people. Always, we must simply believe he will.

> *Be ye angry, and sin not: let not the sun go*
> *down upon your wrath: Ephesians 4:26*

People in the world may not admit it, but they are looking for examples to follow. They are seeking something to believe in again. Will you be that example? Or will you follow the example of the captain who let his anger get the best of him?

We all get angry sometimes. The Apostle Paul tells us about being angry. We were created in the image of God, after his likeness, and we can read in the Bible that God sometimes became angry. If that is so, why wouldn't it be acceptable for us to become angry if we are in his likeness? Because it is not the anger alone that causes problems. It's our actions while we are angry. It is the hurt we create in others when we are angry. It is the time it takes us to get over the anger. All these things take a human and spiritual toll.

If the situation calls for an apology, then apologize. I know it is easier said than done. Sometimes you have to be the bigger person and settle the situation, even though you are the one who deserves an apology. Anytime we do anything outside the character of God, we sin, so we want to be gracious peacemakers whenever possible.

Chapter 8

Journey Home

I wanted to share some excerpts from a book I am currently writing entitled *Journey Home*. I have looked back on my life and all that I have lost and yet God saw fit that I made it through somehow. I hope someone finds some comfort in the book and it helps to encourage them in some way, they come to know Christ, or they realize they can make it no matter what they have been through. That they come to know God is calling them back to Him every day. Life throws us many curve balls and our daily life is filled with waves that can make us feel as if we are drowning. Overwhelming situations can make you feel as if life is not worth living. These situations and overwhelmed feelings cause people to commit suicide every day. If you have Christ, trust and believe in him. Understand he is with you and can bear any burden you place on him.

In 1984 I moved from my mother's apartment in Chicago to live with my uncle in a beautiful small town north of Chicago called Zion, Illinois. The town had streets named after the books of the Bible. I thought this had to be a remarkable place. It happened to be the place I received Jesus Christ as my personal Lord and Savior.

I had no idea what that meant at the time. All I knew was I wanted a different life than what I experienced growing up in Chicago. I had seen people live and die in the same project building in which they were born. I had seen what hopelessness looked like from a very young age. I would often ask myself, "Is this all life had to offer?" I lived my life in Chicago as if everything depended upon me making it to the next day, as if there was no hope, and I would always be nothing more than a screwed up kid from the projects with a less than a meaningless life.

Some people escaped that life through sports, some landing sport scholarships or scholastic scholarships, which was great. Although I played football and basketball in high school, I never imagined getting out because I was not committed to sports.

As I began my new start on life as a Christian in Zion, I could feel something in me changing, maybe because I wanted to change the way I felt about life. I write this part for all high school kids who do not think they have what it takes to make the grade. When I was in Chicago, I consistently made C's, D's, and the occasional F in high school. I never imagined making A's, but when I began to pray at night, read the Bible more, and believe that, Christ dwelling in me made me a better person, I started to focus on a better life. I wanted to represent Christ, so I studied hard and spent lots of time in the library reading.

It paid off. I made the honor roll a few times. I read in the Bible about "renewing of the mind" and I wanted that. I figured I had to renew my mind, change the way I saw my life and what I thought about myself. When I began to believe I could do what I once believed I could not do, I discovered I could do it. I was so proud to have achieved such an honor. It was a high point in my life, along with making the basketball team.

We may think we are hopeless and trapped in hopeless situations. But God can change all that. If we allow ourselves to be open to accept what we see, he could change our vision of ourselves. When we believe, we can change and achieve. Such visions help us mature and become better equipped to handle the future no matter what may come. God wants us to grow and learn.

I eventually graduated high school and joined the Army. Right out of boot camp, I went overseas. I was young, and had never been far from home, let alone another country. I was to be there for two years, but ended up staying four years. I loved Europe and had the opportunity to travel, embrace the culture, and meet some very nice people. My second year I started attending services at the chapel, still holding on to faith.

I had many disappointing moments. I could not understand why God allowed me to see so many situations I thought were "a mess." The Army only had a few chaplains to hold services for a couple of denominations, so a few religions shared the same service. Those services were solely up to an individual to attend or not. Because I possessed a vast amount of knowledge about the Bible, I sat back and watched most of the time. I heard talk of Baptists and a few others, but I had not studied any religious history, so all I could say was I was a Christian that was pretty much all I knew.

Once I came into the knowledge of Christ, so many things I did not understand in the past made absolute sense to me now. I understood how many times I came close to dying, hit by a car at seven years old, nearly drowned at 10, four car accidents, two of which were bad, one so bad it momentarily stopped my heart. I now look back and think how many times Satan tried to take my life. I believe he wanted to prevent me from having a positive impact on the lives of others that was only possible though the knowledge I gained through my relationship with Jesus Christ. I think on how many times I wanted to commit suicide because of depression. If this book impacts one life, draws one person to Christ, or encourages someone to continue their walk with the Lord, then the effort is worth it.

While deployed to Iraq, I had some life changing experiences. I lost my father to cancer prior to deploying to Iraq. I did not attend the funeral because when I finally received word of his passing it was already too late. By the time I would have flown home, the funeral would have been over as we were preparing to deploy. My father and I were not real close, though we would speak on occasion. I would often hunt him down to see if he had any concern for us, his kids. He was never there for my brother or me. Our sister saw more of him than we did because my mother separated from him when we were small. He had an abusive nature and he loved drinking and women. I recall a few months prior to finding out he had cancer. I had this strong urge to visit him. I did not know why, but it was on my heart to see him. So, one day I drove to visit him in Chicago at his small apartment where he lived alone. He had lost so much weight I did not recognize him. He looked so feeble.

My father was surprised to see me. We sat and talked for a while. He asked me for money. I remember telling him that I did not have much, but he was welcome to what I had. Suddenly this feeling came over me and I said, "Daddy I forgive you. I have held a feeling of desertion because you left, and I felt you wanted no part of our lives except if it was too your advantage. You have other kids that you make time to see when you can, yet you make no attempt to see us. But I want you to know that I still love you, I want to be free from this feeling of anger I had been holding against you."

After that, I tried so hard to recall all the things he had done and I couldn't. It was weird. My father looked down the entire time. He could not look at me, because if he had I would have been looking directly into his eyes. He starting crying and said he was sorry. He said he was ashamed of how his life had turned out. He said my mother did not want us around him, and I knew that was true. My mother understood the broken promises he would make and not keep would only hurt us more. We often hoped he would show up, as we were excited to see him. She would constantly remind us of how he would care for his other kids, and would care for us too if he loved us.

I could tell my words had touched him in a deep way palpable even to me. We both ended up hugging and crying together. It was what we both needed. I felt I could get on with my life knowing I had reconciled with my father. I talked with him a few more times and we shared some laughs before he passed away.

I was so glad I made the trip to talk with him. Forgiveness is so powerful, I cannot begin to express how powerful it is. A few months after the passing of my father, I received word my mother had died. I was shocked because she was still young in my eyes. I was convinced the officials who broke the news had made a mistake. I wanted to believe it was a huge mistake, especially since the initial message I received stated both my mother and brother had died.

I had just returned from a mission in the city of Baghdad, Iraq and was told I needed to see the Command Sergeant Major right away. He told me I needed to go to the Red Cross office. I walked in and was hit with the news. I could not stand afterwards. I remember sweating and trying to get ahold of myself. I kept saying, "No, this has to be a mistake." But it was true. My mother was gone and I had no idea of what to do.

The night I received the news I went back to my tent. I sat on the ground thinking and crying. Then I began to talk with God. I still had not accepted my mother's death in my heart and I began asking the one question many ask after the death of a loved one: "God, why did you allow this to happen?" I remember saying to him "You brought me all the way to Iraq to fight for my country, and then you took my mother away. How can that be?"

Yes, I know how foolish that seems, but it's hard to say what anyone would do in the situation. I had a friend who once told me, "Things are never more real than when they happen to you." I thought I had it together too. I loved God and I knew he loved me. He had kept me and those around me safe from harm, yet here I was questioning him about something he already knew.

I was to be on a plane the next day to fly home and bury my mother. It was undoubtedly the hardest thing I ever had to do in my life. No one could understand my demeanor, not even my family, as I arrived home and proceeded to arrange, along with my uncle, for her burial.

My family had no idea what I had been through in Iraq. I somehow felt cold inside, not allowing myself to feel anything. I thought God owed me an answer for the loss I suffered. I remember saying to God, "You owe me an answer. I want to know why she had to be taken from us. She was still young when she died." I knew she was healthy, so I kept thinking something had to have happened to cause her to have a heart attack.

We held a funeral service at her church in Chicago and buried her at a nearby cemetery. With so many things left to do before returning to Iraq, I felt now was not the time mourn her death, more or less I felt I had to be strong and hold everyone else together. So, I hid my feelings. I remember thinking, "I cannot return to Iraq with so much on my mind, because I could make a mistake and get someone killed." I took no time off and returned to overseas acting as if everything was normal.

Chapter 9

Watching over Us

While in Iraq, we constantly faced difficult challenges and situations. We had no idea about the outcome. I cannot count how many times we received incoming bomb attacks during the middle of the night. I prayed late at night and early in the morning on a daily basis. Can you imagine waking up 3am in the morning, getting dressed, and not knowing where you will be heading to for the day? All I knew was that I had to be packed and ready to go by a certain time every morning.

I worked as the maintenance liaison, assisting our commander. My boss insisted I stay close to him. The commander respected my opinion and often asked for my advice. I thought it to be strange he would ask advice from an enlisted soldier. We spent practically 80 percent of our time traveling to meetings and visiting our subordinate units.

I can recall the strange feelings I would have on certain days when I arose in the morning, but I would never acknowledge my feelings to anyone unless I knew I needed to. Often we would face unknown dangers, not knowing if we would be killed that day. I recall one morning when we were riding down a main road leading to the highway and we pulled over to look at suspicious activity near an abandoned vehicle on the side of the road. We got back in our vehicles and started back down the road, when we heard a loud explosion a little further up the road. We later received a radio call informing us there were dead bodies on the side of the road. Apparently, the explosion had been the result of some Iraqis trying to plant a roadside bomb and it detonated accidentally. It came over the radio that if we had been 10 minutes sooner we probably would not have been so fortunate. I took that to mean that if we had not stopped for the few moments to investigate the suspicious activity, we may have been hit by the Improvised Explosive Device (IED). After passing the bodies on the road, I realized the bomb was most likely meant for us.

I also realized we were under God's protection, because God does care for his own. It was not happenstance that saved us, but the grace of God. I was so overwhelmed by what God had done that the joy inside was unspeakable. No one could understand the peace I felt or why I was so upbeat most of the time. My faith in God was so high no one could tell me my God did not love me and or he did not watch over his children.

Knowing how much joy God has brought into my life as I do, makes me want everyone to experience what I have experienced. I want them to see and feel what I feel. Then, the answer to a question like "How do you keep the faith in the mist of so much turmoil?" becomes another question. That question is, "How can you NOT keep the faith?" God saw fit that I made it out of Iraq alive. I'm not sure how well I was mentally, but I had made it out. I had no idea that it could be months, even years before you realize how much of an impact combat has on you.

I ended up leaving Iraq early, so I handed over my tent, my refrigerator, air conditioner, and everything I had bought that made my tent a home away from home. Approximately four days after I left, there was a Rocket Propelled Grenade (RPG) attack late one night. One of the rounds from that attack landed directly inside the tent I left. From what I was told, the impact destroyed everything inside the tent and would have killed me

instantly had I not departed early from Iraq. Again, I could not
do anything but fall to my knees and thank God once I received
that news. I could not get over the realization that if I had not
departed early, I would have been asleep in that tent when the
RPG exploded.

The other blessing I thank God for is that the individual
I handed everything over to when I departed Iraq was not
harmed. God knew what was coming and the guy had worked
the nightshift that particular night and was not in the tent when
the RPG hit. Now tell me how much of a blessing that is! If
something had happened to the guy, I think I would have felt
a lot of guilt. He was a nice and helpful guy, which was partly
why I left him the tent and all of the amenities I had acquired
during my deployment.

I still think about what would have happened if I had not
departed when I did. Do I think the attack still would have
happened had I stayed? I am not sure. I do know my faith has
increased because of that incident.

I believe Satan wants to prevent as many people as he
possibly can from getting to heaven. His attempts start as soon
as you are born. The Bible says Satan is roaming like a lion
seeking whom he may devour. Since he cannot be omnipresent
and omnipotent like God is, he has to roam and seek people
to prey on. The minute he finds an opportunity for evil to
triumph, he inserts himself into the situation. He cannot be
everywhere and he does not know all things like God, but for
him it does not matter. His desire is to distract and confuse you
long enough that you do not see what Christ has to offer you
before you pass away from this earth. Satan knows God cannot
violate his word, so those who do not accept Christ will not be
able to call heaven their home.

I think Satan's biggest deception is having people believe
there is no God. I understand that God has given us the human
power of choice, and some people choose to believe in nothing,
I can only assume Satan has deceived them. I would rather
die believing in God than burn in hell forever. The Lake of

Fire does not sound like the best of places, if you know what I mean. I am not attempting scare tactics here, just expressing an opinion.

I have not made the Christian life sound like a cakewalk, because at times it is not. It has not all been easy. I have lost both my parents, witnessed and experienced some horrible things in Iraq, am suffering from Post-Traumatic Stress Disorder (PTSD), which I believe is responsible for my periodic nightmares of the worse kind, and nearly lost my house. I even wanted to commit suicide on numerous occasions. It was as if I had reached a point where I was losing or about to lose everything. But God was faithful and he gave me strength and hope though all the difficult times.

Chapter 10

Healing

Are you suffering from *post-traumatic stress disorder* (PTSD)? If you have been through traumatic events that sometimes cause PTSD, GET HELP! I was diagnosed with PTSD, but I remained in denial about having it for two reasons: first, I thought I was too "macho" to have it and, second, I thought people with faith in Christ could not get it. However, I can now see how war affects a person. I think anyone who goes to war with a belief system and has a respect for life will undergo emotional changes when they routinely see people killed or seriously injured. To witness someone being shot, and not being able to do anything about it, changes you.

I recall going for knee surgery shortly after returning from Iraq. I had to have screws placed in my knee. They had to put me to sleep before the surgery. After it was over, the nurses told me I was having a flashback as I was coming out of the anesthesia. I was yelling and screaming, "Help that man over there, we have to help him! Please, please help him!" They say I was trying to get out of the bed to help the man I saw in my mind, even though I was fresh out of surgery. If a person will do that, what does that say about PTSD? It is a reminder that IT'S SERIOUS!

The nurses were crying as they calmed me down and restrained me in the bed. I vividly recall some of what was happening in the hospital, but some of it is very blurry. In my mind, I can see the old man being shot in the street in Baghdad and other events that took place that day. It was as if it happened yesterday.

Do not think you can tackle PTSD alone? It has a way of fooling you into thinking you can figure it out for yourself, but just when you think your mind is settled, the trauma returns. When that happens, you can potentially lose your family, friends, and end up destroying your life and the lives of those around you. You don't want to hurt those who love you and those who are reaching out to you help, but that is what often happens. They may not understand what you have been through. Their natural reaction is to reach out to you, because they love you and are concerned. Their actions are gestures of love and you need to accept that love.

It is amazing what the devil will use against you at a time when you are so vulnerable. For example, I started thinking long and hard about my sister who died in a fire. She was about two years old at the time and I was about four or five years old, definitely the age where you need adult supervision. Though as a child you never think about supervision. She died in a fire after my father left us in the house alone. I felt as if it were my fault. I felt that my mother held deep anger towards me because of my sister's death, even though I knew my mother loved me. I have held that guilt nearly all my life, but it increased a hundred-fold I believe because of PTSD.

Can you imagine thinking everyone in your family secretly hated you because you thought they blamed you for a loved one's death? I had to seek help and spend a lot of time praying, but not before turning away people who were concerned and loved me. I remember praying that the Holy Spirit would bring to my remembrance life as I knew it before. I wanted the Spirit to reveal the "real me" and to help me understand what was happening in my life. As I hoped, God brought people into my life that helped me. They guided me back to the right path. It was important for me to know there were still fine people in the world.

There were some very scary moments back then. I associate much of what I lost in the later years of my life to my denial of having PTSD. I did not immediately realize some things about me had changed. Things that would not have normally bothered me easily angered me. I became easily upset. Sometimes I would be very silent. I would normally say a few words to show some effort to communicate with people around me. Sometimes I was non-responsive altogether. I stopped communicating with my few remaining family members— my brother and sister, and my aunt and uncle who helped raise me. I was trying to deal with too many things, including the death of my mother, which hit me very hard emotionally. No one seems to teach us about how to handle our grief, and I guess I never knew how to do that.

All I knew about my mother was that she was gone and I missed her very much. I would sometimes sit in the corner and cry. It felt as if something inside me was missing. When you are so close to your parents and other family, it is hard to accept you will not see them again here on earth. Today, if I meet someone who speaks negatively about their parents, I tell them to reconcile with their parents if they have the chance. I remind them that there may be a time when they realize they want or need them, and they may not be there.

The emptiness left behind by the death of a parent is hard to fill. I'm not saying it can't be done, but most people periodically feel a sense of guilt because they didn't make peace when they had a chance. Parents may not be perfect—they are people who make mistakes too—but they should not be beyond forgiveness. The forgiveness is not for them, but for you. When you forgive them, you can move on without negative emotions hindering your progress in life. Understand some will accept your forgiveness and some may not, but though they may continue to act in the same matter and continue to do what may have caused you to feel the way you do from the beginning, but you have forgiven them. That is the key thing. My father changed somewhat after we had our conversation, but I know every case is not the same. Nevertheless, it's worth the effort. You will see that words of forgiveness are powerful.

How do I continue to be as strong as I am with everything I had been through? How do I keep my head? It is not a simple task, I tell friends who ask the question. However, I can't speak enough about how glad I am that I started believing God a long time ago, and that has made the difference in my life. Although I still have my moments of doubt or lack of understanding, I know in my heart that God will do what he says he will do. I know he will never desert me. I know his mercy endures forever and he is never out of my reach. I can talk with him anytime I want. Most of all, I know that he truly loves me! He loves you just the same, so never think that you are out of reach of God's love.

I have spoken with people who have declared they do not think God loves them. Whether we admit it or not, we have all questioned God's love at some point in our lives. Usually we question God's love based on some event that has taken place. Some of us believe God could never love us, or love us again, because of what has happened in our past.

That assumption is far from the truth. It does explain, however, the reason why so many feel they must or have to get their lives in order before they can come to Christ. I have individuals say, "I need to get something sorted out before I can come to Jesus." However, if they would listen to themselves, they might rethink that. How can you get it right without Christ? How can it stay right without Christ? If you get it right, then you will have to be the one to maintain it. If you get it right with the help of Christ, then it has a better chance of staying right. It's like the old saying "When I get rich and successful I will come back to help others." The idea is that you have to get rich first before you can help someone else make it. The problem I have with that way of thinking is success sidetracks most unsaved people. They get too caught up in their new life to make a serious impact on those they said they would go back to help. I believe the percentage of people helping people is higher for those who have accepted Christ and are living for him.

Chapter 11

Straight Talk

You can help others simply by starting where you are, even if you are living on the streets and have nothing at all. The place you live does not disqualify you from helping someone. I am not saying that you have to settle for where you are, but I am saying you can help others no matter where you may be. Not having money does not disqualify you from helping others. We have drifted away from doing the little things that matter. You could do something nice for your neighbor, for example. It may not require money, but it will probably require time. Time is one of the most precious gifts on earth you can give.

Stop looking for some mighty way to do something—just get back to the basics. Reach out where you are and give from what you have. Trust and believe God will give it back to you. One of the gestures I practice when I go out for dinner with friends or family is to pay the bill and let the others leave the tip. Someone once told me I would never have to worry about a meal. He said God would always ensure I had food on my table because of the way I blessed others with a meal. I can say it has been true to this day, and I am by no means a materially rich man. I am rich spiritually, and that's the most important thing. Sadly, Satan and the wickedness of this world have disrupted the way some people think, and have caused much distrust and confusion. Kind gestures were once common, but now people second-guess the intentions of those who still believe in kindness.

> *"For though we walk in the flesh, we do not war after the flesh: (For the weapons of our warfare are not carnal, but mighty through God to the pulling down of strongholds) Casting down imaginations, and every high thing that exalteth itself against the knowledge of God, and bringing into captivity every thought to the obedience of Christ." — 2 Corinthians 10:3-5,*

I believe it is the church that holds the key to keeping the evil and wickedness of this world at bay. When I say "church" I mean believers; they make up the church. They are the ones who have the spiritual awareness to recognize actions of the devil and his imps who operate within the spirit realm. Christians must initiate periodic offensives to break down whatever evil Satan is trying to put in place. Spiritual warfare can be something as simple as a prayer. If God places something on your heart to pray about, you need to do that and then take action as needed. Although we may not see the results of our prayers all the time, we know prayer will accomplish its intended purpose.

Knowing that gives all of us hope and confidence like nothing else does. It is powerful to know that God's Word will not come back without having accomplished what it was set out to do! We should all be jumping for joy about that. God's Word works. If you are a believer, you should already know that, but if you are reading this book for the first time or because someone recommended it to you, then listen: Gods Word works! You have to have faith to believe it.

> *So shall my word be that goeth forth out of my mouth: it shall not return unto me void, but*

it shall accomplish that which I please, and it shall
prosper in the thing whereto I sent it. — *Isaiah*
55:11

That is powerful! God acts on his Word. It may sound crazy
to some, and I know this because I have been criticized when I
mentioned it in the past. I use to remind God what he said in his
Word, and people would say God already knows what he said
in his Word. He does not need you to repeat it back to him. I
would say, "Are you sure? How do you know?" The whole intent
of quoting God's Word back to him was to let him know that I
know what he said, and that I believe what he said.

Be prepared to put that trust and belief to the test, because
you will face challenges. I have often found holding on to that
Word, and placing it back before God, gives me favor with God.
That leads me to believe that when you want to find favor with
God, you have to gather up the strength to endure things like
unjust treatment, character assassination, and personal attacks;
they will come eventually. Satan has to try to destroy your
character if he is to have any real impact on you.

One of the most striking, tragic stories in the Old Testament
is about King Saul. If we are sensitive to the supreme values and
vital issues of the human life, then his story is bound to challenge
you in some way. It amazes me, for example, how people can say
someone is a good man today, and then tomorrow say he is the
worst form of life. Has the one man been divided or have we
separated aspects of his character? As Christians, it is important
for us to look at the totality of a man. Judging is the way of the
world, and God will hold us accountable if we judge others.
We know the way of the world is not the way of Christ. Don't
react to the attacks. Do not attempt to seek revenge under any
circumstances. That is one of the most dangerous actions you
can ever take.

No one is immune to attacks. It can even happen to the
most prominent and influential Christians in the world. They
may conduct revenge in a more subtle way that is not apparent,

but that has as bad an impact as if it was conducted in an open forum. You know revenge has to be something serious when you understand that God kept it for himself.

> *Dearly beloved, avenge not yourselves, but rather give place unto wrath: for it is written, Vengeance is mine; I will repay, saith the Lord.*
> — *Romans 12:19 (KJV)*

> *Never take your own revenge, beloved, but leave room for the wrath of God, for it is written, "VENGEANCE IS MINE, I WILL REPAY," says the Lord.* — *Romans 12:19 (NASB)*

Revenge is not for Christians. People have started wars over revenge. One act of revenge could last for generations. Sometimes revenge causes countries to fight, and sometimes it causes families to fight. Most family members might not know why the battle rages. There is no such thing as a small act of revenge in the eyes of God, especially when God says, "Do not take revenge." What we may consider a small act of revenge could lead to something we never intended it to be. I believe that is one reason why God withholds it from us. Acts of revenge take a huge human toll in the world we live in. Thus, we have to be wary of what we allow to enter our hearts. When I hear stories about people getting even with someone, I know someone has taken the wrong road and will learn a hard lesson.

If you believe in your heart that God is with you—if you would be still and know that God is with you—you can be confident no weapon formed against you shall prosper. You can know that no man has the power to make you feel as if you are nothing, unless you give that power to him. I cannot stress that point enough. When you fall prey to this, it will make you feel like the place you are in is the place you belong, when that is not necessarily true. On the surface it makes you think your life is meaningless, but in your heart you have a tingling. You know deep down that there is more to you than where you find yourself in one particular moment in time.

> *For as he thinketh in his heart, so is he: Eat and drink, saith he to thee; but his heart is not with thee.* — *Proverbs 23:7 (KJV)*

What do you think of yourself? That's an important question. The content of your heart, and how you understand what is there, is the source of your emotions and actions. The thoughts and intents of our hearts motivate us. That's why we hear so many beautiful testimonies of former street people about how they escaped poverty. They had a true heart.

I have been shocked to realize the amount of talent on the streets, not just in the United States, but in other countries as well. It's amazing and sad at the same time. I have stopped to talk with people on the streets in different countries, and some of the stories I have heard bring tears. Some of these people could be an asset to a corporation if given the opportunity to work. I would challenge any company to engage some of these people and test their ability against what they know of the talents they possess.

Chapter 12

Your Opportunity

If you are not saved, if you haven't made the decision to accept Jesus Christ, you have the opportunity now to accept Jesus Christ as your personal Lord and Savior. Christ is the one who willingly paid the ultimate price for our salvation. He did it so we would have a chance at eternal life. Good works cannot save you and will not get you into heaven. It also does not take a ritual to be saved. You can be saved right where you are, in your home or in a plane at 30,000 feet in the air. Confess with your mouth and believe in your heart that Jesus Christ is the Son of God. He died on the cross for your sins and mine; he rose from the grave on the third day, and is seated at the right hand of God.

Once you know heaven is your home though Christ, you can be sure spiritual opposition will come. Satan does not want you to make heaven your home. You don't have to be the perfect person to go to heaven. Trust me, I am far from being perfect; we all are works in progress. Grab and read the instruction manual for life, the Bible, for yourself. I cannot stress that enough. Get a Bible and read it. Ask God to help you to understand what you are reading. Also, ask God to lead you to an excellent church where you can learn and grow. Allow God to give you ideas, dreams, and plans. He wants you to find new meaning and renew your excitement about life.

When you do find the church, remember you are going to hear what God is saying to you. He may not be speaking the same thing to the person seated next to you, but that's okay. Don't make the mistake of becoming discouraged by focusing on the events inside the church rather than your intentions for going.

God may allow you to see certain things so you can pray about them. While attending service at a base overseas, I was asked to be the driver for the pastor of the church who was a single parent. I did not know him very well, and I was young. There were rumors this pastor had a relationship with the woman who was the nanny for his kids. The pastor did not speak about the rumor, but he never denied it. One Sunday I was picking him up at his house for service, and while waiting for him I would periodically look at the house. With one of the glances I saw him kissing the woman I assumed was the nanny.

I could not believe my eyes. It was something I was not supposed to see, I thought. I felt I was not to say anything to anyone about it. I automatically assumed that he had broken some great spiritual law. I had judged and condemned the man without hesitation. I was scared for some reason when he came out. Because I thought he saw me through the window, I was thinking, "What do I say if he asks me what I saw?"

After reaching the church and going inside, it was impossible for me to get anything out of the service. I only thought about what I had just seen. I also judged and condemned the nanny who attended the same church. I thought, "Wow, they have tried to keep this a secret and now I know the rumor is true." My best friend at the time was a deacon at the church. After the service, he would always ask me what I got out of the sermon. This particular morning, I did not have any answers, no comments, nothing.

To let you know how serious this affected me, I did not attend service for a few weeks and I used the excuse that we were preparing for a field exercise. The only problem with that is my best friend and I was in the same unit. I would try to avoid him at all cost during the duty day. He found me, as he always would, and suggested we go to lunch together and I agreed. Of course, he asked me what was going on. I said nothing except I had a lot on my mind and was trying to figure out some things. He said, "What better place to work them out than church while hearing what God had to say about it?"

I wanted to say, "Hey I really don't want to have anything to do with that religion stuff." You see, something I saw physically had sidelined me spiritually. Not once did I think what I could possibly learn from seeing what I saw.

What was the result? I did later go back to church and to my surprise that very day they announced the pastor was engaged to be married to his kids' nanny. Apparently, they had been engaged for some time, but wanted to keep their life private and announce their engagement when they were ready. Now, imagine how I felt— I was relieved and at the same time ashamed at how I reacted to the whole incident. God showed me something about myself and those around me—mostly myself. I told myself that I would never ever react or prejudge anyone again. You can say its human nature, but I tell you it is controllable.

Those feelings cost me time, affected my emotions, and sidelined me spiritually. I can almost say I was obsessed with the obvious—it looked like they were sleeping together while not married. She lived with him, he was the pastor of the church, and that was a problem to me. However, I learned I had to be careful because I had no idea what was taking place inside his home.

When God did create an opportunity for me to talk with the pastor, I found out that we had things in common. We were from the same hometown, knew the same families, and were friends with them. We ended up having some hearty laughs and I felt that he was a very caring and sincere person. After speaking with him, the peace I had made me want to go to church to hear what God had to say through the pastor. I was open to receive from him again. I tell you, God knows how to put the finishing touches on an ending.

The truth is the battle of life we are fighting has already been won. Christ paid the ultimate price so we did not have to do that ourselves. Our responsibility is to continue to have faith in God. We must continue to fellowship with him and let him know how we are feeling. He already knows our hearts and he reveals things we don't understand. Get to know yourself. The more you know about yourself, the easier it is for God to use you and the easier it is for you to access and face reality.

Obedience is the secret to having a great relationship with God. I have heard many different ideas on what happens after you become saved and try to live your life for Christ. Some people say your spiritual battle begins when you first trust Christ. Yes, you will face many hard challenges, and things will seem complicated, but God will take care of you. Obedience is always the key to a victorious life in Christ.

Some people may tell you that you should be much further along in your walk with Christ. I tell them it is not a race. The roads we travel will sometimes divide, and, if you are running, you may rush down the wrong path. You could run far down the wrong road before you notice it gets narrower and has no light. That's when you need to stand still and wait on God. Be patient and let him work his perfect work in you.

Whatever you do, don't feel discouraged because you see someone else moving fast or going past you. Trust and believe God will get you where you need to be. Notice I said, "need to be," and not always want to be. Sometimes our wants do not line up with God's will for us.

Sometimes the road seems to end because of the obstacles in the way, so we turn back or stand still. I believe sometimes God wants us to travel down the road with obstacles. He has lessons for us to learn on that road. I take it one day at a time, staying focused and listening for guidance. What do you do in the absence of instructions from God? Read and study your

Bible, pray, and get out and put the word to work. As you begin to recognize the gift God has given you, use it to bless others; do not use it for your own personal gain. Trust me it happens! We hear the term "being in the flesh," which describes how people sometimes use spiritual gifts for personal gain, something that is always wrong to do.

Self can interfere with your fellowship with God, can cause you to miss your blessings, and even take your life. It's like a cancer. When we are in the flesh, or self, we can easily fail to see our present condition robs us of our spiritual strength and dulls our effectiveness. You do not have to give in to self.

Remember, we are most vulnerable to a failure or defeat immediately after a great victory, so be careful not to let your guard down not even for a moment. Stay "prayed up," as they say. I dedicated a place in my house where I go to talk with God. I can do that anywhere in the house, but I wanted a place that was his and where I could meet him in prayer.

Chapter 13

Acknowledgments

Pray over your house. It works! Thank God for the angels who are encamped around about your house, and then picture angels armed and ready around your house guarding your family. I have done research about angels and I can tell you that you do not want to tangle with them. Keep God first in your life and the Word of God in your heart. Believe in your heart you are destined for great things. It happens to people every day, but so many sell themselves short.

Remember you are the one that complicates your own life. You can deceive yourself but not your heart. Don't waste your time— always be aware that your time is valuable. You should always value the time of others. Learn to appreciate the moment. Once you have learned to appreciate and cherish the time God has given to you, everything you do, and how you do it, will change.

It seems the world has a lot to offer, but never think the world has more to offer than God does. This misconception entraps us. We expend so much energy chasing the world's offerings that it drains us. It's only later we realize that when we do get one of those worldly "gifts" it is not what we wanted. Trust me, I have lived this and can tell you firsthand how it works. Something looks alluring, but it often disappoints. It's like the guy who desperately wanted a big screen TV. It was so big it took up most of the space in the room. He sacrificed a few things to get the TV to fit. It later developed some problems and it ended up gathering dust in that same room where he placed it on the day he brought it home. He would brag on the TV, but he never had time to enjoy it. The world does not have more than you do—as a Christian you have more than enough if you would just tap into it.

I want to take a moment to say thank you to God for creating me and revealing to me the importance of following his purpose in my life, and for his relationship and fellowship. I want to thank him for making the ultimate sacrifice in giving his only begotten son, Jesus Christ, who paid the price so I might be saved and have eternal life.

I thank my loving mother, whom I love so much, for her many sacrifices and hard work to provide for our family. I have not forgotten the many lessons she taught me. She has gone home to be with our Lord, but I still miss her so much. I know I will see her again.

To Bishop Anthony McMillan, who has always been my father in the faith, a mentor, and a friend, thank you so much for the straight talk.

Reginald Tate is a man who treated me as a brother. He was closer than my blood brother, shared with me what brotherly love should be, and was an example to follow.

Luther Scott, my uncle, has been a great influence in my life and he has always been there for me. I do not think I would be the man I am today if it were not for his display of love for God. He inspired me to say to myself, "I want to love and seek God the way he does." His untiring love for family has helped us all stay in communication with each other. My Aunt Nellie Scott, who stands by his side and supports him, has been an example of what qualities to look for in a wife. She is a beautiful person and a blessing to me.

To the men of God who have shared their wisdom and some instances imparted knowledge in some form, I thank you. God has allowed me to cross the paths of many other people and we have learned from each other. I would like to say thank you to each of them. I hope we have been an encouragement to each other and will carry what we have learned from each other through our walk of life.

I try to look for the good in everyone. Even if the person has overwhelming problems, you can find one quality that you like about him or her, learn from it, and take it with you. We all have to learn to get together and remain the kind of people God has created us to be. I believe it can be done, and that it must be done, if we are to be a people with the purpose of fulfilling God's calling. We should have it set in our mind that while not everyone will make it to heaven, we are not the decision makers and that every life is worth trying to save.

To those whom paths I have yet to cross, I pray for you even before we meet. My prayer is we will be open to receive whatever it is God has planned for us to receive from each other, even if it is simple fellowship. I pray that our minds are open and our ears attentive to what the Holy Spirit has to say, and that it touches our hearts.

To my readers, thank you for purchasing this book. I hope you will find it and any future books encouraging. I pray you will share it with someone along your travels through this world. I will continue to pray for you and ask that you pray for me as we live out our purpose on earth together. Pray that we can make a difference in this world and reach out to those in need, draw the lost to Christ, and let the world know that Christ is very much alive in us. Together we can teach others to dig into their untapped potential and help them realize they have a purpose.

One thing I would ask God to do is help people focus on the important things in life. I did not understand the importance of breaking off those things that were not of God, no matter how much it hurt me, or how much pain it would cause me. When I stopped doing spiritually unprofitable things, I was able to focus on things that matter. I learned that lesson and I pray others will learn it too since it will impact every aspect of their life.

I pray for my fellow veterans who may be suffering from PTSD. The first step in getting help is acknowledging you need it. My advice is that you listen to your family. They may not understand what you are going through, but they recognize your actions are not the actions of the person they know. It is so important to start fighting your way back to them. It is a slow process and there is no overnight cure. You may still experience some nightmares, but when you awake, you realize that's all they are. Nightmares can be a periodic occurrence in the life, something to accept with grace. If you continue to be in denial of this illness, it can cause you to lose everything you love. No one is immune from PTSD, and part of its deception is for you think you are normal or have no issues.

There are organizations like the Department of Veteran Affairs that have group sessions to help those suffering from PTSD. These groups share their stories and the pain of what has taken place within their lives. They provide guidance about how to cope with making it back to some form of a normal life. Getting this help is important because some stages of this illness can be dangerous to yourself or those around you. I am not sure why it causes dysfunctional behavior in some and not in others, but we all react differently in certain situations. I would become easily angered, sometimes inflamed, over small things. It seemed as if every emotion had been intensified ten times over. If I was sad, I would be very sad and if I was angry I would be very angry. It was often difficult for me to control my emotions.

Although PTSD took a toll on me, I thank God I did not end my life. God brought people into my life who helped me realize I could talk to them and I remain in contact with some of them today. They brought with them positive messages and always encouraged me to look to God for healing, giving him the glory for it. That brought me the peace I needed, and I found myself slowly making my way back. There is no cure for PTSD, but you can get better by keeping your distance from negative people and living a positive life.

"Purpose draws potential, potential brings to life Destiny. Understanding you have a purpose is the first brick on the road to Destiny!" — Otis Teague

Salvation is a Done Deal!

Printed in the United States
By Bookmasters